—— Stuff Every ——

GOLFER

—— Should Know ——

© 2015 by Quirk Productions, Inc.

Library of Congress Cataloging in Publication Number:
2014948251

ISBN: 978-1-59474-799-1

Printed in China
Typeset in Goudy and Franklin Gothic

Designed by Andie Reid
Production management by John J. McGurk

Quirk Books
215 Church St.
Philadelphia, PA 19106
quirkbooks.com

10 9 8 7 6 5 4 3 2

—— Stuff Every ——

GOLFER

—— Should Know ——

By Brian Bertoldo

QUIRK BOOKS

PHILADELPHIA

To my mother and father

Thank you for the love, support, and encouragement you've given to me over the years

Introduction

Much has been written about the grip, the stance, and the myriad dynamics of the golf swing. You'll find an endless stream of advice in print and online about how to cure the many golfing ills, such as the slice or a hook. However, many of the less-mechanical nuances of the game—stuff like etiquette, history, and the dos and don'ts—are most often passed down from golfer to golfer. These pieces of advice and wisdom are the soul of the sport.

This book is a selection of some of this "stuff" a golfer should know, rather than *everything* a golfer should know. The pages that follow describe those elements of the game often learned through interaction with other golfers, not from golf pros or swing gurus. Sometimes these are extremely practical things; other times they are simply fun facts or the stuff of 19th hole banter. Either way, it's all stuff worth knowing.

Whether you're new to the game or a veteran low handicapper, my hope is that you'll come away with some worthy tidbits to pass on to your golfing partners while you're out on the course this weekend.

ABOUT THE GAME

How Old Is the Game?

Here's a thorny question to start things off. It is generally accepted that the game we recognize as golf has been around for at least 600 years. As with any centuries-old game, however, its true origin is shrouded in mystery.

Ancient Roots

Dating back at least to the Roman era, people have been playing stick-and-ball games. Over time, most if not all such early sports have faded from the playing fields. Today, we have plenty of other stick-and-ball games—baseball, softball, hockey, even billiards, to name just a few. And, of course, there's our beloved game of golf. It seems that folks have always enjoyed whacking something around with a stick!

Popular Enough to Ban

But let's try to stick (no pun intended) with the few facts we do have. King James II made the first written reference to golf in 1457, when he banned the game in the Scottish Act of Parliament. It seems the Scots were spending too much time playing their favorite game instead of focusing on archery practice. Those archers were mighty important in the days when the longbow dominated the battlefield. Many believe the game was being played in Scotland a century or more before the ban, plenty of time to become popular enough to warrant its interdiction in the mid-15th century.

Further evidence of Scottish heritage can be seen with sand bunkers. It's believed that Scottish shepherds brought these elements into the game, much to the dismay of golfers across the ages. The first bunker shot probably occurred when a shepherd's ball fell into one of the hollows where sheep had burrowed through the grass into the sand underneath, most likely to seek shelter from the famous coastal Scottish gales. Thanks to these seaside golfers of yore, we also have links golf—open, mostly treeless courses laid out along the ocean. But, of course, many hated bunkers come with beloved links golf.

Other Possible Origins

So, that's why the Scots have come to be so closely associated with golf's origin. However, it's worth mentioning that the Dutch, with their game of *kolven*, and the Chinese, with a game called *chuiwan*, have also claimed to be originators of the game.

Key Dates in Golf History

1457 King James II of Scotland bans the playing of golf with an act of Parliament.

1552 In a charter dated January 15, 1552, the citizens of St. Andrews, Scotland, are given the right to use land to play golf.

1754 Founding of the Royal and Ancient Golf Club of St. Andrews. To this day, it is the governing body of golf everywhere outside of North America.

1848 The creation of the gutta-percha golf ball dramatically changes the game. A vast improvement over the old "featheries," which were made of a feather core wrapped with a leather cover, the gutta-percha is constructed of a molded rubberlike material.

1860 The first Open Championship (British Open) is held at Prestwick Golf Club on the southwest coast of Scotland. Willie Park edged out Prestwick's greenskeeper, Tom Morris, by two shots to win the tournament with a total score of 174 for 36 holes.

1894 The Amateur Golf Association of the United States is founded. It will go on to be named the United States Golf Association and will be the ruling body of golf in North America.

1895   The inaugural U.S. Amateur and U.S. Open Championships are played at Newport Golf Club. Charles B. Macdonald wins the Amateur, with Horace Rawlins taking home the $150 first prize for the Open.

1916   The Professional Golfers' Association is founded. The first PGA championship, won by Jim Barnes, takes place at Siwanoy Country Club in Bronxville, NY.

1923   A 21-year-old Bobby Jones wins his first U.S. Open at Inwood Country Club in New York.

1927   The first Ryder Cup match is played at Worcester Country Club in Massachusetts. The U.S. team beats Great Britain 9½ to 2½.

1930   Golf's dominant player, Bobby Jones, becomes the only player to win the Grand Slam by taking home first place in the U.S. Open, U.S. Amateur, British Open, and British Amateur. The 28-year-old Jones retires from the game.

1934   In what would later be renamed the Masters, Horton Smith wins the first Augusta National Invitational.

1946   The first U.S. Women's Open is held at Spokane Country Club in Washington. Patty Berg takes home the title the first and only time the tournament is played in match play.

1950   Thanks to the efforts of 13 pioneering female golfers, the Ladies Professional Golf Association (LPGA) is founded.

1953   Ben Hogan nearly wins the modern
        Grand Slam with his victories at the Mas-
        ters, the U.S. Open, and the British Open.

1960   Arnold Palmer has a banner year by
        winning eight PGA Tour events, the
        Masters, and the U.S. Open, plus sec-
        ond place at the British Open.

1965   Gary Player wins the U.S. Open, becom-
        ing the first foreign-born player to do so
        in decades. He donates the majority of
        his prize money to promote junior golf.

1966   Jack Nicklaus takes first at the Masters,
        winning his third green jacket, and
        his second in a row. His victory at the
        British Open this same year makes him
        only the fourth player in history to win
        all four majors.

1968 Winning 10 tournaments each, Kathy Whitworth and Carol Mann dominate this season's LPGA Tour.

1971 In just a four-week period, Lee Trevino wins the U.S., British, and Canadian Opens, becoming the first player to do so. This year's PGA Championship winner, Jack Nicklaus, becomes the first player to win all four majors twice.

1975 Lee Elder is the first African American to compete at the Masters.

1979 At just 22 years of age, Seve Ballesteros wins the British Open.

1983 Tom Watson wins his fifth British Open at Royal Birkdale.

1986   At age 46, Jack Nicklaus wins his sixth
        green jacket at the Masters, giving him
        a total of 18 major wins.

1997   Tiger Woods becomes a household name
        with his record 18-under-par victory at
        the Masters. This historic win ushers in
        the Tiger Era and gives a needed boost to
        the game's popularity worldwide.

1999   In what would be billed as the "Bat-
        tle at Brookline," the American team
        mounts a final-day comeback to defeat
        the Europeans in the 33rd Ryder Cup at
        the Country Club in Massachusetts.

2000   Tiger Woods wins the U.S. Open at Peb-
        ble Beach by a record 15-stroke margin.
        Subsequent victories this year at the
        British Open and the PGA Champion-

ship make him the first golfer since Ben Hogan to win three majors in a year.

2001   By winning the Masters, Tiger Woods becomes the first golfer to hold all four major titles at one time. This accomplishment would be known as the "Tiger Slam."

2004   After years of being known as "the best player to never win a major," Phil Mickelson takes home the green jacket at the Masters for his first win in a major.

2008   Despite an injured knee, Tiger Woods wins his third U.S. Open title in a dramatic Monday playoff against Rocco Mediate. With this victory, Woods becomes only the second man since Jack Nicklaus to have won each of the majors at least three times.

2010 Northern Ireland's Graeme McDowell is the first European winner of the U.S. Open in 40 years.

2011 Rory McIlroy becomes the youngest U.S. Open champion since Bobby Jones in 1923. McIlroy's 16-under-par total of 268 beats the previous scoring record by four strokes.

2012 Thanks to an amazing hook shot from the trees on the second playoff hole, Bubba Watson wins the Masters.

2013 With his victory at Muirfield Golf Club, Phil Mickelson wins his fifth major and first Open Championship.

Why 18 Holes?

For much of the game's history, golf was played on however many holes the course owners built. Some had just a few, while others had as many as 22 or more. When the first Open Championship (British Open) was played at Prestwick Golf Club in 1860, it was decided that players would play the 12-hole course three times—in the same day!

The Old Course at St. Andrews was the first to establish 18 holes as a standard round of golf. It would take 100 years for it to catch on universally. Originally, the Old Course had 12 holes, with 10 of them being played twice, for a total of 22 holes. Then, in 1764, it was determined that the first four holes were too short, so these were combined to make two. Then eight holes were played twice for a total of 18. Why? Who knows. Some say it's because there were 18 shots in a bottle of whiskey!

In 1857, St. Andrews redesigned several greens to accommodate two separate holes (the now-famous double greens), and in doing so it became an 18-hole course. Conveniently, also around this time, the Royal and Ancient Golf Club of St. Andrews decreed that a standard round should be 18 holes. As the century progressed, clubs wanting to be in line with R&A rules designed their courses to either 9-hole (played twice) or full 18-hole layouts.

Who Was Mulligan?

The mulligan: the classic do-over we remember from childhood games. In golf, the mulligan is an opportunity to erase from memory, and the scorecard, that last awful shot. So where does the term come from? Was there some unfortunate fellow named Mulligan who never seemed to get things right the first time?

Several stories exist to explain this piece of golf trivia. By turning to none other than the USGA for guidance, we can narrow down the number of tales to four. The first three involve a hotel owner named David Mulligan, a golfer who played at St. Lambert Country Club outside Montreal in the 1920s.

The first story has it that Mr. Mulligan started off his round one day with a very long, yet highly inaccurate tee shot. He immediately teed up another ball, as if on the driving range. His playing partners said nothing as Mulligan swung away once more and this time, presumably, found the fairway. Thankfully, everyone was so amused with this little stunt that they named the do-over after him.

In the second story, Mulligan had carpool duties on the way to St. Lambert. After picking up his playing partners, he made a white-knuckled drive along a road in such disrepair that he arrived at the club quite shaken. In sympathy, his friends gave him an extra shot off the tee to calm him down.

In the third story, it seems that one morning Mulligan overslept for his tee time. After waking late, throwing on some clothes, and rushing to the course, he was very much out of sorts on the first tee. Not a good way to start a round. Predictably, his first drive was a dud, so he just teed up another. *Voilà*—a mulligan!

The fourth and last account comes from the Essex Fells Country Club in New Jersey. In the 1930s, the club's locker room attendant was a man named John A. Mulligan. A well-liked fellow, Mulligan would play rounds with club members after work. One day, after an errant shot, he remarked that he should be allowed to replay it because, after all, these gentlemen were out playing all day, whereas he just came from work. And from then on, they called a replayed shot a mulligan.

The use of mulligans can be a sore spot with some golfers, and they're certainly not allowed in competitive play. However you feel about them, there's little chance they'll disappear from the game anytime soon. If a member of your weekend foursome insists on taking a mulligan, here's a way to make it fun. Simply "charge" the player a preassigned dollar value for each mulligan used. The group "collects" at the 19th hole, when it's time to settle the tab!

The Evolution of the Golf Club

Winston Churchill once famously remarked, "Golf is a game whose aim is to hit a very small ball into an even smaller hole, with weapons singularly ill-designed for the purpose." No doubt, many of you out there wholeheartedly agree with this assessment—especially those who have tossed a club into the woods or a pond after a particularly horrendous shot. However, golf clubs have come a long way since Churchill's time. And unfathomable leaps and bounds have been made since the days when Scottish shepherds beat about a wooden ball with their crooks.

The homemade clubs of the sport's earliest days eventually gave way to implements fashioned by bow makers and carpenters as a sideline business. Rather crude by today's standards, most of these early clubs resemble something a caveman might use to bring down a great beast. But as skills developed and the game grew in popularity, the age of the clubmaker was born.

By the 18th century, these artisan workshops were making wooden-shafted playclubs, spoons, and niblicks for the discerning golfers of the day. Though these names and the clubs designed for them have long since gone the way of the wooly mammoth, they are the forerunners of the titanium and graphite equipment we use today.

The really big changes came in the 20th century with the advent of steel and, later, graphite shafts. Gone were the days of easily warped or broken hickory. Improvements in forging and casting gave birth to high-quality irons and wedges with grooved faces for spin control. Drivers evolved from small wooden-headed affairs, to steel models with larger heads, to even bigger titanium monsters the size of a cantaloupe. And let's not forget the putter. For decades the putter's design hadn't changed dramatically; wooden heads and shafts gave way to steel, of course, but the clubhead itself stayed relatively uniform. That all changed in the later half of the 20th century with the introduction of head designs in all shapes and sizes, made of everything from urethane and carbon fiber to space-age alloys, even glass!

The 21st-century golfer has an arsenal of implements that would stagger the minds of the game's earliest players. No doubt if Mr. Churchill were to walk into a pro shop today, he'd think a golfer might have at least a fighting chance against that very small ball.

The Goods on Golf Balls

Few sport balls in the world have had as much research and technology injected into their design and manufacture as the humble little golf ball. Today's golf ball industry is run much like classified weapons projects, employing secret formulations, space-age materials, and corporate intrigue.

It wasn't always that way. The first golf balls were just simple wooden balls. As the game matured, golfers demanded something a little more sophisticated. Bound by the technology of the time, early equipment makers came up with the "feathery"—a core of tightly packed feathers covered with leather. The feathery was difficult to produce and expensive—often times costing more than a single golf club. But, it was the only game in town for over 200 years.

In 1848, the gutta-percha golf ball was invented. Made of a natural rubberlike material from the tropical percha tree, the "guttie," as it was called, made golf balls easier to standardize and more affordable to produce. When damaged, the guttie could simply be heated up and reformed.

Compared to the "feathery," the guttie's reign was short lived. By the end of the 19th century, a man named Coburn Haskell discovered that wrapping strands of rubber around a rubber core produced a ball with remarkable bounce qualities. By covering this wound ball with balata sap, Haskell had created the first modern golf ball. This design was further refined through the early 20th century. Especially important was the adoption of aerodynamically efficient dimples, now so common, on the ball's outer cover. By altering the size, number, and pattern of dimples, manufacturers were able to manipulate distance, spin, and feel around the greens.

By the late 20th century, the wound ball's days were numbered, though to this day, many players still swear by its superior spin characteristics. With the advent of synthetic materials such as urethane, golf balls could do away with wound rubber threads. Today, golf balls are available in two-, three-, and four-piece designs that incorporate layers of high-tech materials to achieve performance characteristics best suited to a golfer's needs.

The more simple two-piece models tend to be the least expensive and cater to the high handicapper, recreational golfer. These balls are tough, have little spin and "feel" around the greens, and are made to go straight and far—great for folks with low swing speeds, not so great for those seeking feel and control.

The three- and four-piece designs are typically better suited for mid and low handicappers. Made of a softer outer core with inner components tuned to provide more spin and shotmaking control, these balls are perfect for the more accomplished golfer who wants to shape shots and have the ball check up on the green. They are really bad for anyone with a wicked slice or hook (whose ball will spin sharply sideways into the next county).

Green Grows the Grass

Everyone knows a golf course is covered in grass. No big news, right? But do you know the different grasses that are commonly found on golf courses? This information is more than just trivia—it could help you with your game. Here are the grass types you should know.

- **Bermuda grass.** Typically found in warmer climates, bermuda grass thrives in heat and humidity and is resistant to drought. It can be used on greens and fairways and to make rough. Bermuda grass fairways will provide a fluffy surface for the ball to sit up on. When used in rough, it's a bugger, grabbing and twisting the club. Bermuda greens can be tricky. When left a bit long, the thick, coarse blades of this grass can slow down the ball, but when tightly mown, the ball's speed will increase.

- **Bentgrass.** This is one type you'll run across most often on greens in cooler climates. Bentgrass doesn't like the heat and will tolerate cold to some degree—better than bermuda grass, for sure. Its thin blades grow close together, making for a dense surface that can be mown very short. That makes for a fast putting surface.

- **Zoysia.** Sounds exotic, right? In fact, it's a quite common grass type and can be used in a variety of climates. It's often used in tee boxes, fairways, and rough. Zoysia is a hardy grass with deep roots and can be clumpy.

- **Fescue.** If you play a majority of your golf along coastal regions, then you've played on fescue. Commonly used for rough, it can grow up to three feet tall. Watch out for this stuff—it loves to grab hold of clubs. Ever hit a shot from the rough and end up with a clubhead covered in a giant bird's nest of turf? That was probably fescue.

- **Ryegrass.** Another clumpy style of turf, ryegrass withstands stress and wear very well. It's often found in cooler climates on fairways and tee boxes. Ryegrass is popular with greenskeepers for overseeding—the process of putting down one type of grass seed on top of the existing growth of another.

- ***Poa annua.*** In northern and cooler climates, this turf type is often used to create greens. A *Poa annua* green is characterized by a spotty appearance of lighter and darker areas, making its surface difficult to read. In addition, it can be a bit bumpy. One famous course with *Poa annua* greens is Pebble Beach.

A final note about grasses: A quick phone call or a visit to a course's website will be able to tell you which ones are used and where. Knowing the kind of grasses you'll be playing on can help you make decisions around the golf course, and it's especially crucial when reading greens.

Who Wrote the Rules?

The time comes in every golfer's life when you would just love to kick the guy who wrote the rules, right? Well, there's no one guy to kick. And even if there were, he'd be long since dead. It is an old game, after all.

That leaves us with the sport's two ruling bodies: the Royal and Ancient Golf Club of St. Andrews (R&A) and the United States Golf Association (USGA). Today, the two organizations work in conjunction to administer the rules of the game worldwide.

Every four years, these two governing bodies jointly publish *The Rules of Golf*. They've been doing so since 1952. Prior to that, the R&A and USGA published their own separate rule books, often similar in substance but varying on small points. The agreed-upon regulations published today consist of 34 rules and some 1,300 decisions that are the same in both the R&A and USGA editions.

The oldest known set of golf rules dates back to 1744, when the Honorable Company of Edinburgh Golfers wrote down a set for their silver club championship. As with today's rules, it's safe to say there were probably some confounding rules in that document for golfers to lament over and gripe about.

But even when you just can't stand the rules, it pays to pay attention to them. For example, among the most often ignored by weekend duffers is the 14-club rule: a player must not start a round with more than 14 clubs. Take a quick look around the first tee and you'll see that some players have so many clubs, their bags resemble multi-tentacled monsters from the deep. In tournament play, the enforcement of this rule can make or break a round. Professional golfer Ian Woosnam found out the hard way at the 2001 Open Championship. He was tied for the lead in the final round when, on the second tee, his caddie noticed there were 15 clubs in the bag! Since he'd already started the round, Woosnam was assessed a crippling two-stroke penalty. That penalty, and the resulting frustration it caused, effectively ended his bid for the Claret Jug. So don't be like Ian

Woosnam—be sure to count your clubs before each round!

Note: If you're playing a new course, be sure to consult the scorecard or check with clubhouse staff to learn about any quirky rules concerning their particular layout.

The Majors

The four main professional men's championships held each year are collectively known as the Major Championships. The Majors include the Masters, the U.S. Open, the Open Championship (British Open), and the PGA Championship. Winning any one of these is a tremendous accomplishment in a pro golfer's career. Victory also fetches a hefty paycheck (low seven figures), tons of media attention, and lucrative endorsement offers worldwide. It's life changing. And then there's the Grand Slam—to win all four majors. That is the holy grail of golf. Bobby Jones is so far the only player to win a Grand Slam. In 1930, he won the U.S. Open, U.S. Amateur, British Open, and British Amateur, the four Majors of that era.

The order of play for the four modern Majors is the same each year:

- The Masters: the second week of April

- U.S Open: third week of June

- Open Championship: third week of July

- PGA Championship: third week of August

The Masters

If anything could be called a cathedral of golf, it would be the course at Augusta National. This timeless stretch of Georgia landscape is the creation of Bobby Jones and the architect Alister MacKenzie. Like the tournament played there every spring, it is revered the world over. The Masters has been an iconic golf event since its inception in 1934. In addition to more than a million dollars in prize money, the winner takes home the prized green jacket, which is ceremoniously presented to him by the previous year's winner.

Major Facts:

- The Masters is the only major to be played on the same course each year, and it is the only one to use a sudden death playoff in a tie.

- It was originally called the Augusta National Invitation Tournament; the name change to the Masters Tournament was made in 1939.

- Bobby Jones would finish no better than 13th in his 12 appearances at the tournament he founded.

- One of the most famous shots in golf history happened at the 1935 Masters, when Gene Sarazen hit a double eagle, bringing him into a tie for first place and forcing a playoff, which he won. It became known as "the shot heard 'round the world" and is credited with helping bring the Masters tournament into prominence.

- Jack Nicklaus has won a record six Masters victories. Arnold Palmer and Tiger Woods tie for second place, with four wins apiece.

U.S. Open

The second-oldest of the four modern Majors and the second to be played each year (in June), the U.S. Open is universally known as a grueling test of skill and nerve. Like the Open Championship and the PGA Championship, the U.S. Open is played at a different course from year to year (most are private, but public courses have hosted, notably Torrey Pines and Bethpage). Suffice it to say the courses chosen are always among the most beautiful and challenging in America (e.g., Pebble Beach, Winged Foot, Pinehurst). And the USGA, which runs the Open, loves to tweak the layouts to raise the level of difficulty. One of their favorite additions: punishingly high rough.

Major Facts:

- The first U.S. Amateur and U.S. Open tournaments were played in 1895. At the time, the Amateur was the more popular attraction, with the Open relegated to sideshow status.

- Four golfers claim the top spot for most U.S. Open wins: Jack Nicklaus, Willie Anderson, Bobby Jones, and Ben Hogan each have four victories.

- The last amateur to win the U.S. Open was John Goodman, in 1933.

- The tournament's first winner, Horace Rawlins, took home $150. The 2014 champion, Martin Kaymer, claimed a record $3 million.

- Oakmont Country Club, in Oakmont, Pennsylvania, has hosted a total of eight U.S. Opens, the most of any course.

The Open Championship

Known as the British Open in the U.S., the Open Championship is the oldest Major, dating back to 1860. It is played in July, with the venue changing from year to year, though always on a links course. Currently, the rotation consists of Carnoustie, Muirfield, Royal Birkdale, Royal Liverpool, Royal Lytham & St. Annes, Royal St. George's, Royal Troon, St. Andrews, and Turnberry. The location tends to alternate roughly between courses in Scotland and courses in England. The Open Championship is the preeminent championship tournament. For the golfing world, it's like the World Series, World Cup, and Super Bowl rolled into one.

Major Facts:

- St. Andrews holds the distinction of hosting the most Open Championships, with 27. Prestwick (no longer in the rotation) is a close second, with 24.

- Greg Norman's winning score of 267 at Royal St. George's in 1993 is the lowest in Open history.

- Harry Vardon holds the record for the most Open Championship victories, with six between 1896 and 1914.

- The last amateur winner was Bobby Jones in 1930.

- Since 1873, the winner receives the famed silver Claret Jug, whose official name is the Golf Champion Trophy.

PGA Championship

Hosted by the Professional Golfers Association of America, the PGA Championship is the final Major of the year and is played in August. Begun in 1916, it was created as a national championship for professional golfers at a time when amateurs dominated the game. Perhaps not as well known as the other three Majors, the PGA Championship is still a stern test of skill. The host course changes from year to year and has included such famed layouts as Valhalla Golf Club, Oakland Hills, Medinah, Riviera, and Congressional.

Major Facts:

- In 2000, Tiger Woods became the first back-to-back winner of the PGA since Denny Shute in 1937.

- The winner receives the Wanamaker Trophy, named for Rodman Wanamaker, a department store magnate who hosted the first meeting of the PGA.

- The format was changed from match play to stroke play in 1958.

- In addition to a hefty paycheck, the winner of the PGA receives a lifetime exemption into the PGA Championship and five-year exemptions for the Masters, U.S. Open, and British Open.

- It is the only Major not to invite amateur players into the field.

LPGA Majors

The Ladies Professional Golf Association has its own collection of majors—these are the women's marquee tournaments. Over the years, the number of majors on the women's tour has varied. Today, there are five: the U.S. Women's Open, the KPMG Women's PGA Championship, the Women's British Open, the Kraft Nabisco Championship, and the Evian Championship. In addition, these three events were formerly classified as LPGA majors:

- The Women's Western Open was played from 1930 to 1967 at a different course each year.

- The Titleholders Championship was played from 1937 to 1942, then from 1946 to 1966 and again in 1972. The host course was Augusta Country Club, next door to Augusta National.

- The Du Maurier Classic was a major from 1979 to 2000. It is now called the Canadian Women's Open but is no longer a major.

In the history of the LPGA, two players have won the single-season Grand Slam. In 1950 Babe Zaharias won the three majors at that time: the U.S. Women's Open, the Titleholders Championship, and the Western Open. In 1974 Sandra Haynie won the two majors played that year: the U.S. Women's Open and the LPGA Championship. So far no player has won a five-major (or four-major, when there were four official majors) Grand Slam.

U.S. Women's Open

The oldest of the women's Majors, the U.S. Women's Open got its start in 1946 when it was conducted by the Women's Professional Golfers Association (predecessor to the LPGA). It wasn't until 1953 that the USGA took over the event. The women's Open is played on a different course from year to year. Previous host courses include Oakmont, Newport Country Club, Salem County Club, Colonial, and Hazeltine, to name but a few. It is considered the preeminent event in women's golf and is open to both amateurs and professionals who qualify.

Major Facts:

- The first U.S. Women's Open in 1946 was the only one to be played at match play. Patty Berg beat out Betty Jameson, 5 and 4, in the 36-hole final.

- Just 37 players competed in the 1953 Women's Open. In 2014 the field consisted of 156 contestants.

- There is no upper or lower age limit for qualification. In 1954 Babe Didrikson Zaharias becomes the oldest champion in the history of the event, winning at age 43.

- Betsy Rawls and Mickey Wright share the record for most wins, at four a piece.

- In 2014 international qualifying was introduced at sites in China, Japan, England, and Korea.

KPMG Women's PGA Championship

Previously known as the LPGA Championship, this is the championship event for the LPGA and the second oldest major, having gotten its start in 1955. Like the men's PGA championship, it is open only to professional golfers.

Major Facts:

- In 2005 the LPGA allowed an amateur, 15-year-old Michelle Wie, to play in the championship—the only instance of an amateur being invited into this event. (Wie competed the next year as a professional.)

- It is the only major that legendary professional golfer Nancy Lopez won during her career. However, she did win it three times!

- The championship was formerly known as the Wegmans LPGA Championship; the name was changed in 2015. It has also been known as the LPGA Championship and the McDonalds LPGA Championship, among other variations.

- The 2015 event was the first time the PGA of America and the LPGA teamed up to hold a women's major.

- Previous winners include Mickey Wright, Betsy Rawls, Kathy Whitworth, Nancy Lopez, Juli Inkster, Annika Sörenstam, and Se Ri Pak.

Women's British Open

The history of the Women's British Open dates back to 1976, but only since 2001 has it been recognized as a Major by the LPGA. The venue changes each year and has included such notable courses as Royal Lytham & St. Annes, St. Andrews, and Royal Birkdale.

Major Facts:

- It became an LPGA Tour event in 1994.

- The current corporate sponsor is Ricoh. Officially, the full name of the event is the Ricoh Women's British Open.

- It is organized by the Ladies Golf Union, the governing body for women's amateur golf in Great Britain and Ireland.

- Karrie Webb and Sherri Steinhauer are tied for most victories in the Women's British Open with three each.

Kraft Nabisco Championship

This tournament has been around since 1972, when it was founded by entertainment icon Dinah Shore. The championship has always been held at the Mission Hills Country Club in Rancho Mirage, California. It wasn't considered a Major by the LPGA until 1983.

Major Facts:

- Typically held in late March or early April, it is the first LPGA Major played each year.

- In recent years, it has become a tradition for the winner and her caddie to jump into Poppie's Pond on the 18th hole.

- Since 1983, three golfers share the top spot for most wins, at three a piece: Amy Alcott, Betsy King, and Annika Sörenstam.

- The tournament was formerly called the Nabisco Dinah Shore; it is still strongly associated with the late TV talk-show host and longtime supporter of women's professional golf.

The Evian Championship

Formerly known as the Evian Masters, one would think it had always been considered a Major. It wasn't until 2013, however, that the event was recognized as such by the LPGA. It is the last women's Major to be played each year (in September) and is always held at Evian Golf Club in Évian-les-Bains, France.

Major Facts:

- Evian Golf Club sits on the picturesque shores of Lake Geneva.

- It began as a tour stop on the Ladies European Tour in 1994.

- Ranked as one of the richest prize purses in women's golf, it has offered over $3 million in prize money in recent years.

- Helen Alfredsson has the most wins on record, with three. Annika Sörenstam and Ai Miyazato have each won twice.

Attending a PGA Tour Event

Cheer with the gallery when a crucial putt is sunk or watch in awe as a monster drive flies overhead. The sights and sounds of a live professional event cannot be replicated on TV. Plus there's food, drinks, and bathrooms to boot! Sponsors set up booths with games, kids' zones, and giveaways (free stuff!). And if you're in the know, you might even get into one of the corporate viewing boxes.

Tournament Tips

- Some events do not allow cell phones. Check before you go. Even if phones are permitted, be sure to turn off the ringer.

- One of the best times to attend is during the mid-week practice rounds. Few spectators show up, and the players are usually a little more relaxed, so you may even hear them joke among themselves.

- If you're attending multiple days, choose the first day to follow a group or groups. Walk the course, taking it all in. Along the way, scout out a few good spots to watch from and then spend the next day there, watching the groups come through. You'll get a fuller experience this way.

- Definitely check out the driving range. The best time to go is at the end of the day. The golfers are usually going over some fine details with their swing coaches and aren't as "in the zone" as they would be before the round. There are usually some opportunities for autographs and maybe a chat. Just be respectful and know that some players are all business, whereas others will sign items and talk a bit with spectators. Wait to approach until a player is leaving the range or taking a break near the ropes. Do not do any of this out on the course!

- Rules concerning bags and other items are always changing. Typically, backpacks, coolers, and large chairs are prohibited. Check the event's website beforehand for specifics.

- Be sure to check the weather forecast ahead of time. Don't get caught without an umbrella! And bring sunscreen and a hat—there's usually not a lot of shade to be found in the gallery areas.

- Stay behind the ropes and follow the instructions of tournament marshals. (When the marshals raise their hands for quiet during a player's shot, be sure to cease talking and be respectful.)

- Get cash ahead of time. Though some concessions at the venues take plastic, it's a good idea to have money on hand. When portable ATMs are available, the lines are long and the fees steep.

- Wear comfortable shoes! You're going to be walking—a lot. Oh, and don't run—they really frown on that.

GOLF
LIFESTYLE

How to Keep Fit: A Few Golf Exercises

For a long time, golfers were thought to have a fitness level slightly above a bowler's. That all changed in the late 1990s with the advent of the Tiger Era and the resulting fitness boom in the sport. Hitting the gym became necessary to be competitive. That mentality soon trickled down to amateurs and weekend duffers alike.

It's important to know which areas of the body to focus on and how best to work them. Golf fitness is not about lifting massive weights; it's about building flexibility and endurance.

Upper Body

If you've got shoulder problems, you can't golf. To improve shoulder strength, attach an exercise band to a doorknob or other secure point of about the same height. Sit in a chair facing parallel to the band and grasp it with both hands (simulating a golf grip) at about the midpoint of a backswing. Rotate your arms and shoulders as one piece away from the band's anchor point. Do 10 to 15 reps. Replace the band with a stronger one as you improve.

Another good exercise is the Shoulder Blade Squeeze. This one you can do pretty much anywhere. Stand up straight with your hands at your sides. With your chin tucked in a bit, bring your shoulders back and squeeze them slightly. Avoid the urge to arch your back. Hold for 5 seconds and repeat 10 times.

Middle Body

Bad backs have kept golfers off the course for years. Try the Wall Squat to keep the lower back (and hips and legs) strong. Stand with your back against a wall and your feet shoulder width apart about a foot away from your body. Keeping your back against the wall, lower your knees to a squatting position (about 45 degrees). Hold this position, tensing your abdominal muscles, for 10 seconds. Return to standing and repeat.

Lower Body

Keep your legs toned and you won't have to worry about them quitting on you the next time you opt to walk your favorite course. The exercise called the Step-Up is a great leg strengthener, and the only piece of equipment needed is right in your home—a step! Start by stepping up with one leg, bringing up the rest of your body and your other leg. Hold for a moment, then step down with the opposite foot to your starting position. Repeat, alternating leading legs each time.

The feet are often the most neglected body parts when it comes to fitness. But they are the foundation of everything golfers do. This exercise is called the Golf Ball Roll; it's great for relieving plantar fasciitis or heel pain and keeps the foot flexible and less prone to injury and fatigue. Sit in a chair barefoot with a golf ball under your foot. Roll the ball back and forth under the arch of your foot for two minutes. Repeat with the other foot.

Note: If any exercise becomes painful, stop immediately. Always consult your physician before starting any exercise regimen.

Office Golf: Tune Up Your Game While at Work

Demanding jobs, family, and the business of everyday life can make it difficult to practice and be ready for a weekend round. All too often we rush to the course a bit early in the hope of hitting a few balls at the driving range or the putting green before teeing off—as if this will somehow exorcize the evil gremlins hiding in our swing! Well, truth is, there are ways to squeeze in a bit of practice on the sly during the workday.

Practice Putting

Bring your putter, and a few balls, to work. This is one facet of the game you can practice almost anywhere there's a carpet and a target to hit. Smooth out your stroke in between phone calls or when you get back from a bathroom break. Just a few putts a day aimed at a strategically placed coffee mug can go a long way. A lunchtime putting contest is a great way to get the competitive juices flowing, and it promotes office moral!

Practice Short Chips

Speaking of lunchtime, get outside for a bit, especially if there's a grassy area nearby. Keep a wedge and a bucket of old balls in your trunk. After eating your sandwich, practicing hitting some short chips using the bucket as your target. Even if it's for 15 minutes, that little bit of practice time will pay off around the greens come the weekend.

Exercise

Do some golf-related exercises at your desk (see page 64). Staying strong and limber is always going to help your game.

Golf for Work

Here's one that must be "played" with caution: Golf has always been closely associated with business. So, if your job involves sales or marketing, a midweek nine-hole round with a golfing client could be good for the company's bottom line. Just be sure the bosses are okay with it—and don't win (your client will appreciate this). Use it as a practice round.

And speaking of bosses, golfing on the sly is a whole lot easier if your boss is in on it as well. Cutting out two hours early to squeeze in nine holes before dinner is great fun when the boss leads the way out the door!

How to Calculate Your Handicap

Math! Yes, it's part of the game. Knowing your USGA Handicap Index can make the game more enjoyable when playing with or against players of differing abilities. Your home club may track it using a calculating system, and online calculators are available as well. But what do those numbers mean? At first glance, calculating your index resembles an equation for sending a satellite into orbit. But I'll try to put it as simply as possible.

These are the basics of calculating a handicap index if you do not already have a handicap. Consult the USGA's website (usga.org) for specifics about maintaining a handicap because you will be using Adjusted Gross Scores for the equation. For this example, we will use the USGA system and assume 10 rounds of golf have been played.

1. Subtract the USGA Course Rating for your home course from your score. For this example, let's say your course's rating is 72.5 (your

course's scorecard will display this number) and your score for the first round was 95.

$$95 - 72.5 = 22.5$$

2. Multiply that number by 113 (the slope rating of a course of average difficulty).

$$22.5 \times 113 = 2542.5$$

3. Divide that by your course's slope rating (also found on the scorecard). Let's say your home course's slope rating is 124. This is your Handicap Differential for the first round.

$$2542.5 / 124 = 20.5$$

4. Repeat steps 1–3 for each of the 10 rounds played. Then take your lowest three Handicap Differentials and average them. (The USGA has a chart you can use to determine the correct number of Handicap Differentials based

on the number of scores you have; three is the correct number based on 10 rounds.) Let's say your lowest three Handicap Differentials are 19.5, 20.5, and 21.4.

5. Take the average of your three lowest Handicap Differentials.

$(19.5 + 20.5 + 21.4 = 61.4) / 3 = 20.466$

6. Multiply the average by .96.

$20.466 \times .96 = 19.647$

7. Delete all numbers after the tenths digit.

19.6

That number—in our example, 19.6—is your Handicap Index.

What to Wear

Fashion trends come and go—and some have a knack for coming back around, for better or worse. Well, the same goes for golf fashion.

Shirts

Sure, you could wear the same old cotton solid color polo that everyone wears. It's a golf staple, for men and women. Stripes are good, too. Or slip on a form-fitting, stretch panel polo in the most outlandish color imaginable! It's what the pros are doing these days. Mock turtlenecks are also good, whether long-sleeved or short. Just leave the T-shirts at home. Most important, wear something comfortable that allows you to have a free range of movement. It's all well and good to look sharp, but if you can't swing your club, then what's the point?

Pants

Please, no jeans. Yes, they fly at some public courses, but this is golf, not yardwork. Bottoms with slits have come back from the '70s, as have plaids and a variety of funky prints. Pleats are out; flat fronts are in. Be aware that areas of golf courses may be wet and muddy. So avoid pants that are too long, or you'll be dragging around wet and dirty cuffs all day. For the ladies, skirts are always in fashion, but don't forget a belt! Wide belts with bold, solid colors and big buckles have been the rage for the past few years. Have some fun with it. Shorts are usually acceptable in the warmer months. Just be sure to check the dress code before arriving at each course.

Shoes

Proper golf shoes are a must-have for both fashion and practicality. The golf shoe is the anchor of your swing, so get a well-fitting style that will grip the turf. If the classic saddle shoe is your thing, you're in luck—those are still around. But you may want to try the athletic styles that abound today. They look and feel like sneakers but do everything a good golf shoe should do. And, no, regular sneakers are not appropriate for the course. For classic golf style, don some argyle socks or make a statement with a pair that's brightly colored or fancifully patterned.

Gloves

Gloves are more than just apparel; they're an equipment choice that protects your hands from blisters and prevents club slippage, thus improving your game. Manufacturers are constantly experimenting with materials, designs (seams, closures, etc.), and technologies to improve efficiency and performance. Styles are available in leather or synthetic blends. Most important is to get the proper fit—beware of choosing too large, a common mistake. Go to a pro shop or sporting-goods store that offers a good selection and try on several pairs till you find the one that fits, well, like a glove.

Hats

Covering up your noggin' is a good idea, especially if you're folically challenged (like me). The baseball-style cap has become the standard for both men and women, but the old-school slouch cap or even a bucket hat (great for rainy days) are equally good choices.

Sunglasses

Even if it's a cloudy day, bring along a pair. It's better to have them and not need them than to need them and not have them. Glare from water hazards, bunkers, and even freshly mown turf can be as distracting as bright sunlight.

Golf Bag
Essentials

It's a bag; it's got lots of pockets. So fill it with
stuff, right? Here's a list of must-haves to help you
be a little strategic with the load you have to lug
over hill and dale.

AN UMBRELLA	Because rain shows up when you're least prepared for it.
A SMALL FIRST-AID KIT	Cuts, scrapes, and insect bites happen on the course. Sunscreen and insect repellant are good additions as well.
A SMALL CLOTH BAG	This will come in handy for loose change, keys, wallet, watch, and such, keeping them all in one place.
EXTRA PENCILS, TEES, AND BALL MARKERS	Because, like socks in the laundry, they just seem to disappear.

BRUSHES	No, not for your hair, for your clubs and shoes. A clubface brush will keep the grooves clear of dirt and debris, and a shoe brush will aid in getting the same out of your cleats. It works for goose droppings as well.
TOWELS	Notice the plural here. You want one to wipe down your clubs and one for you. Don't mix them up.
A BALL MARK REPAIR TOOL	Few things are as frustrating as a green that looks like the face of the moon. Fix your own ball marks as well as any others around it. It's just good practice to pay it forward.
SNACKS	Whatever snacks you like, be sure you've got them squared away before your round. Word of advice: If they go uneaten, don't forget about them afterward. An old banana smooshed in a bag pocket makes for an unwelcome surprise. And bring fluids, too!

Five Winter Tune-Up Tips

For players living in regions with long golfless winters, it's hard to keep your mind, body, and swing in shape for when the robin sings and the fairways defrost. So here's some helpful advice to keep you motivated and prepared for the season to come.

Exercise

Yes, it's tough to do when it's below freezing outside and the recliner, the TV, and a plate of nachos are calling. But resist! Any work you do during the winter months to stay flexible and strong will pay off big in the spring. You don't have to pump iron at the gym. Stretching, yoga, and simple resistance band exercises are just as effective, perhaps even more so.

Swing Away

Yes, slowly swinging a weighted club or your heaviest iron for a brief period each day can keep you limber and thinking about your swing. Just make sure that if you practice indoors, you have enough room to swing freely. Your spouse will not appreciate club marks on the ceiling!

Focus on the Short Game

Putting and even short chip shots can be practiced indoors. Inexpensive putting mats are available at pro shops or online. Or just place a coffee mug on the carpet and aim for that. For chipping, it's best to use plastic or foam practice balls and an old piece of rug to hit from. And watch that backswing! Grandma's vase might be right behind you.

Use Your Imagination

Sports psychologists have been advocating the practice of visualization for years. Of course, envisioning yourself exercising probably isn't going provide any benefit; however, visualizing a perfectly hit drive or a solid approach shot will. Playing these over and over in your mind will instill confidence, plus it's a nice way to daydream on a snowy day.

Read

Yes, what you're doing right now. Read golf magazines and books, and visit golf-related websites. Study the game and its history. Use the off-season to learn how to straighten that drive or improve on some other weak area of your game. You've probably been told before that golf is at least 50 percent mental. Well, give your brain a workout!

What to Watch: 5 Golf Movies

Like many sports, golf has served as the motion picture backdrop to comedies and dramas alike. And how fitting—a typical round of golf contains a rollercoaster ride of emotions. Here's a selection of some of the most beloved golf movies.

Caddyshack (1980)

This modern classic is one that golfers and non-golfers alike know and love. Thanks to the comedic talents of director Harold Ramis and stars Bill Murray, Chevy Chase, and Rodney Dangerfield, you're going to laugh, a lot. A selection of quotes from this movie can still be heard on golf courses today. "Be the ball!"

Tin Cup (1996)

Every wonder what goes on with the pros behind the scenes? Here's a lighthearted look at just that. Kevin Costner stars as a struggling pro golfer trying to get back in the game and win the girl, played by Rene Russo. Cameos abound, with appearances by Phil Mickelson, Fred Couples, Peter Jacobson, Jimmy Roberts, and more.

Happy Gilmore (1996)

Many golfers love this movie; others, mostly the purists, not so much. It's an Adam Sandler creation, so you know what you're in for. Sandler, a freakishly powerful hockey player, joins the PGA Tour to save his grandmother's house. Ever hear anyone yell, "Get in the hole!" at a PGA event? That gem, like many other one-liners, comes from this movie.

The Legend of Bagger Vance (2000)

This is one for the Zen-loving golf spiritualists out there. A member of World War I's "lost generation," played by Matt Damon, spends years in an alcohol-fueled depression before agreeing to play in a tournament against Bobby Jones and Walter Hagen. A mystical caddy named Bagger Vance (Will Smith) appears to help Damon's character overcome his golf and life demons.

Bobby Jones: Stroke of Genius (2004)

A biopic on the life of the late great Bobby Jones, the film follows Jones's journey to win the Grand Slam. Along the way, he must grapple with a fierce temper and a tendency toward perfectionism to achieve what is considered the game's greatest accomplishment.

Golfing Presidents

Many of the nation's chief executives have played golf, especially during America's golfing boom in the early twentieth century. Woodrow Wilson, Warren G. Harding, and William Howard Taft were all known to retreat to the fairways for a little R&R. Thanks to a love of the game and a respectable handicap, a few modern presidents have been closely linked with the game, as well.

Dwight D. Eisenhower

Ike loved golf so much he had a putting green built just outside the Oval Office! There was even a tree named after him at Augusta National, off the 17th fairway. The naming honor wasn't due to any great golfing feat the president may have performed at the venerable course, however. It seems the tree so confounded Ike's game that he lobbied to have it removed—unsuccessfully.

From then on, it was known as the Eisenhower Tree. Ike might be happy to know that it fell victim to a storm in 2014 and has been removed.

George H. W. Bush

At one time an 11-handicapper, the elder Bush is American golf royalty, of sorts. A member of the World Golf Hall of Fame, he is also honorary chair of the USGA Museum and Archives President's Council and an honorary member of the PGA. His grandfather, George Herbert Walker, a former president of the USGA, was responsible for creating the Walker Cup tournament. Former senator Prescott Bush, Bush's father and also a former USGA president, was a frequent playing partner of Dwight D. Eisenhower.

Bill Clinton

Introduced to the game at age 12, William Jefferson Clinton brought a new level of cool to presidential golf with his cigars and jovial playing style.

His playing partners often included well-known celebrities from the sporting and entertainment worlds. It is said that Clinton got his handicap down to 10 during his presidency, a fact that has been hotly disputed. It seems that Mr. Clinton is a big fan of taking a mulligan or two, sometimes on a single hole! Presidential privilege, no doubt.

George W. Bush

"W" is said to have played 100 rounds of golf during his presidency—no record but still amazing, considering he gave up the game for much of his first term to concentrate on the wars in Afghanistan and Iraq. Like his father (above), the younger Bush is a capable golfer. His mother, Barbara Bush, does not approve of some of the language he uses out on the course!

Other notable golfing presidents include Franklin D. Roosevelt, John F. Kennedy, Lyndon Johnson, Richard Nixon, Gerald Ford, Ronald Reagan, and Barack Obama.

Golf Travel Tips

You've got your flight, hotel, and tee times booked, and that golf vacation you've dreamed of all year is just days away. What more is there? Here are a few tips to make that trip even better.

- Make a list of all the equipment used in any given round, from tees to ball markers and everything in between. Cross them off as you pack. Don't forget useful items like an umbrella, rain gear, and sunscreen. It's a bummer to show up without equipment and have to replace it at the inflated prices charged at most course pro shops.

- If you don't already have them, buy a second pair of golf shoes (and break them in ahead of time). Rain, mud, and perspiration could leave your primary pair in bad shape for the next day's round. A back-up pair may prove to be a godsend.

- Pack your clubs extremely carefully. Invest in a good travel cover, preferably a solid case. If you're using a soft travel cover, wrap the club-heads in foam padding or bath towels. As an added precaution, some golfers will insert into the bag a broom handle or similar length of stick, slightly longer than the clubs; this will absorb any blows to the top of the bag. Use available space wisely—store shoes, clothing (great for padding), and anything else you might need in the travel cover. And don't forget a luggage tag!

Renting clubs at your destination is another option. You won't have to worry about your own clubs being damaged in transit, and it's a great opportunity to try out equipment you may be interested in purchasing. Individual courses and resorts often offer this service. Well-known golf destinations (Myrtle Beach, St. Andrews, etc.) will usually have club rental agencies in the area. Just call ahead, making reservations if needed.

• If you're not already staying on the course, such as at a resort, be sure to get directions ahead of time. You don't want to be rushing around in the morning or risk being late for your tee time!

- If you're paired up with local players, be sure to ask them for the lowdown on any quirks about the course layout and find out the best places to eat and hang out after the round.

- Many higher-end and resort courses offer the services of caddies. If you've got a little extra dough, it's usually worth it. You'll get the lay of the land and advice on shots and club selection, plus you'll be helping out a local trying to make ends meet.

- Don't overdo it. Trying to cram 36 holes a day into a three-day outing is not advised for most folks. Know your limits and plan your tee times accordingly.

Golf Destinations

Here's a selection of the top popular golfing spots for when you're eager to take your game on the road.

Myrtle Beach, South Carolina

With more than 100 courses running along the South Carolina shore, Myrtle Beach is a golfing mecca. And if you're traveling with family, there is plenty to keep them occupied while you're on the links. In addition to the 60-mile-long sandy beach, there are amusement and water parks, restaurants, theaters, nightlife, and outlet shopping. Many of the area's resorts offer stay-and-play golf packages, so be sure to look into those. Must-play courses include the Dunes Club, the Legends courses, Barefoot Resort courses, TPC of Myrtle Beach, and Caledonia Golf and Fish Club.

Pinehurst,
North Carolina

The very name has a mystical aura. It's where the famed course architect Donald Ross carved a masterpiece into the Carolina Sandhills, and where the late great Payne Stewart won the 1999 U.S. Open in his characteristic stunning style. Bobby Jones once called Pinehurst "the St. Andrews of American golf."

Pinehurst Resort is home to a total of nine courses (the resort owners recently purchased National Golf Club and renamed it No. 9), but it's No. 2 that gets all the glory and attention. That's where Stewart won and where other titans of the game have tested their mettle.

Four choices of accommodations are offered in "The Village," as the resort is called, which boasts a world-class spa, dining, and family activities to boot.

St. Andrews, Scotland

Visiting St. Andrews may be akin to a pilgrimage more than a vacation. With nearly 500 years of golf to its history, it is a must-play for the serious golfer. Most associate it with the famed Old Course, but St. Andrews Links also offers six other courses to enjoy, so there's plenty of golf to keep you busy.

In your off time, be sure to explore the town, home to one of the oldest universities in the world, the University of St. Andrews (also famed for its royal alumni). Don't miss out on a tour of the ruined medieval castle and 11th-century cathedral. A pint of ale or a dram or two of Scotch at the Jigger Inn, just off the Old Course, is a must.

Pebble Beach, California

Dramatic views of the Pacific Ocean, whales breeching in the bay, and ancient forests little changed by time—such is the natural setting for a magical golf course. Pebble Beach Golf Links has been host to the U.S. Open five times and is perhaps the preeminent American public golf course.

The resort's golf academy can help any player improve, regardless of skill level. Other notable courses in the area are Spyglass Hill, rated one of the toughest in the world, and the Scottish links-style Spanish Bay. (The latter features a bagpiper who closes the course according to tradition.)

But Pebble Beach takes the cake with its stunning cliffs, sweeping views, and sloping greens. Just be sure to bring you're A game—it's a beauty, but it's no pushover.

Timeless Golf Jokes

Every foursome has a comedian—is it you? Even if you aren't the witty type, these classic golf jokes are sure to crack some smiles out on the course.

A golfer tees off on the first hole and hits a wide, sweeping slice toward a nearby road. The ball strikes the windshield of a car, causing the driver to crash into a tree. The stunned golfer runs toward the clubhouse shouting, "Help, help! I sliced my tee shot into a car, and it went off the road. What should I do?" The club's golf pro says, "Try a stronger grip."

Frank and Charlie are about to start a round together. Frank says to Charlie, "I hear you had something terrible happen on the course last week."

Charlie says, "Yeah, I was playing a twosome with Joe, and at the ninth hole he dropped dead!"

Frank says, "Someone told me you carried him all the way back to the clubhouse. That must have been difficult!"

Charlie says, "Well, carrying him wasn't that bad. It was putting him down for every shot and picking him up again that was the hard part."

Why did the golfer
change his socks?

He had a hole in one.

Gus and a friend are playing a round one day at their local golf course. Gus is about to chip onto the green when he sees a long funeral procession on the road next to the course. He stops in mid-swing, takes off his golf cap, closes his eyes, and bows in prayer. His friend says, "Wow, that is the most thoughtful and touching thing I have ever seen. You truly are a kind man." Gus replies, "Yeah, well, we were married thirty-five years."

OUT ON
THE
COURSE

Basic Etiquette

Few sports are as demanding as golf in the realm of etiquette. You're probably not going to see a hockey player complain about someone making noise in the middle of a slap shot. Talk during a golfer's backswing or step on their line and, well, that's going to get a reaction. Here are some basic dos and don'ts that all golfers should follow.

Don't make too much noise. If a player has addressed the ball, all conversation and unecessary noise should cease. That player will now have a thousand thoughts circulating about the brain concerning how to get this tiny ball on target. The last thing he or she needs to hear is the rest of your story about last night's escapades or the loose change jangling in your pocket.

Use honors to tee off in order. The player with honors is the one to tee off first on a hole; it's the player with the lowest score from the previous hole. The rest of the players follow according to their score on that last hole. For the first tee, players can draw lots to determine the order of play.

Learn where to stand. Do not stand directly behind a player addressing/hitting the ball. It is preferable to stand across from the player. And be sure to stay still, no fidgeting.

Yell fore! Yes, yell it loud if your ball is careening toward other players or if you don't know where it's going. Don't be ashamed—it happens to us all. And it might save someone a trip to the emergency room.

Follow the golf cart rules. If you're driving a golf cart, be sure to follow the course's specific rules regarding their use. Most clubs will have signage throughout the course directing you where to drive. If nothing can be found, adhere to the 90-degree rule: cross the fairway to your ball at a 90-degree angle from the cart path. And never, ever, drive on the greens or in the bunkers.

Fix your divots. If you make one, fix it. Replace the removed turf and press it down with your foot or use the sand and seed mixture some courses provide on their carts.

Keep up the pace. It's your responsibility to keep up with the group in front of you. Don't take too much time looking for lost balls or arguing over who is away. Of course, don't hit into the group ahead, either! Judge their distance appropriately and keep the pace of play moving.

Rake your bunkers. After a bunker shot, use the rakes provided to smooth out your footprints and the hole left from that last fabulous sand save. When done, rakes should be left facing down and parallel to the direction of play. Also, be sure to enter and exit the bunker at the point closest to your ball.

Fix ball marks. Just hit a perfect approach shot? Great, but be sure to fix that nice deep mark your ball left on the green. To do so, use a repair tool or a tee. Insert it into the edges of the mark and lift the turf. After the edges have been raised, use your putter head to flatten it. If you've got time, fix a couple of the others you see.

Don't step on the line. When on the green, do not walk between a player's ball and its path to the hole. By stepping on the "line," you could alter the turf and adversely affect the putt. If necessary, step over the line as if it were a stream of burning lava.

Drink responsibly. Whether drinking beers on the course or knocking back a few at the clubhouse, it's become part of the game for many players, like it or not. If you do drink, be sure to adhere to the course's rules concerning alcohol and, as always, be responsible. Don't leave beer cans on the course or drive a golf cart while impaired. In fact, my advice is to forego the adult beverages during your round and save up your thirst for the 19th hole. Winner buys the first round!

Playing It Safe

Golf is one of the safer sports out there. No one is crashing into you—or shouldn't be—and you're not jumping or running about, except maybe after an eagle.

Nevertheless, golfers should use some common sense to stay safe while on the course. Here are a few suggestions to make your round as fun and injury free as possible.

Wear sunscreen. As with any outdoor activity, exposure to the sun comes with the game. And with rates of skin cancer on the rise, it's a good idea to wear sunscreen, preferably a type that is sweat resistant.

Wear a hat. Especially in hot, sunny climates, you should shield your noggin from sunburn and as a prevention to heat stroke.

Stretch before your round. Five minutes of simple stretches can go a long way toward preventing golf-related injuries.

Drink plenty of fluids. I mean water or sports drinks. Dehydration adversely affects your ability to play well and make decisions, and it can be extremely dangerous. If you choose to down a few beers during your round, it's important to also drink nonalcoholic beverages to stay sufficiently hydrated.

Bring snacks. With a typical weekend round on public courses stretching to four hours (or more), you will probably get hungry. And when you're hungry, your blood sugar drops, which will make you a terrible golfer. (And it'll probably cause you to be a bit moody, making you a not-so-fun playing partner as well.) A piece of fruit, an energy bar, even peanut butter crackers are some easy on-the-go snacks for the golf bag.

Watch the weather. If thunder or lightning move in, you should move out! Take cover in a designated lightning shelter, permanent building, or car or head directly to the clubhouse if it's nearby. (Use your best judgment about which to choose.) Do not hide under a tree—that is an extremely bad choice (lightning bolts love trees).

Lightning strikes on golf courses are all too common, so take any storms very seriously.

Attend to injuries. Small cuts, bruises, bug bites, pulled muscles, and a host of other minor medical issues can pop up during a round. Use your judgment and decide whether to play on or seek treatment. If a major emergency occurs during the round (think: heart attack, stroke, or traumatic injury), call 911 immediately. We all have cell phones these days. After 911 is contacted, if you know first aid or CPR, put it to use if you feel comfortable doing so. It's wise to alert the clubhouse of the situation as well. Do so for several reasons: many courses have portable defibrillators on the premises; a doctor or nurse might be hanging about; and course staff can help direct EMTs to the site of the emergency when they arrive.

How to Read Greens

On the green, the contours of the landscape will determine where the ball goes. Reading those peaks and valleys correctly is sure to knock strokes off your game. Here's what to know.

Scope out the situation. While walking up to the green, observe how it's built into the landscape. Is it on a hill? Does it have multiple tiers? Take notice of nearby hazards, especially water. Water is a good indicator of how a green drains, which in turn reveals the direction of its slope.

View your putt from different angles. Get down low and move around your ball. Viewing from the downhill side will help you determine the slope. Viewing from the rear will aid in figuring out the break. Side views can reveal subtle hills and valleys as well as the severity of the slope.

Break a long putt into a series of smaller putts. Read the segments separately, and then formulate a plan to get your ball through each one, starting from the hole and extending back to the ball. Combine them, and you've got your line figured out.

Determine the direction. Uphill and downhill putts are going to break differently. Because an uphill putt will be struck with more power, momentum will likely cause it be less affected by the break. So, line yourself up accounting for less break in an uphill putt. For downhillers, the opposite will apply. Because a downhill putt will likely be struck with less force and have less momentum, it will be more influenced by the break. So, line yourself up accounting for more break in a downhill putt.

Read the slope. A putt across a side slope presents its own challenges. What's different here is that the first part of the putt will be uphill, whereas the second half will be downhill. Properly gauge the severity of the slope and the speed needed, and you'll be fine.

Don't overthink it! Once you've made up your mind on a line to take, step up and go for it. Indecision or second-guessing will only result in wasted time and possibly a blown putt. And endlessly circling a putt will frustrate your playing partners.

Wet Weather Golf

So, you've got a tee time booked and rain is forecasted, or you're on the fourth hole and the sky just opened up. What to do—call it a day? No way! Follow these tips, and you'll be ready for whatever Mother Nature throws down on you.

Note: We are assuming that no thunder or lightning is present. If either starts, get off the course immediately. Remember the scene in *Caddyshack* where the Bishop gets zapped by a bolt from heaven? Yeah, you don't want that.

Also, many courses have a horn or alarm that is sounded when lightning is detected in the area. If you hear it, pack it up and seek shelter.

Be Prepared

- Bring along the rain gear, even if the forecast has only a slight chance of rain. Keep wet-weather items in the trunk of your car at all times, ready to go. Gore-Tex brand rain suits are expensive, but they're worth it. They are waterproof and breathable, which means that perspiration, and the fabric, won't stick to you. An inexpensive pair of slip-on nylon pants and a packable rain jacket work well, too. Don't forget an umbrella—the bigger, the better. They're not called golf umbrellas for nothing.

- Even if you don't regularly wear a golf glove, keep some wet-weather ones tucked away in your car or golf bag. They're sold in pairs and will help you maintain your grip in even the wettest conditions. You don't want that new wedge to go flying out of your hands into a pond, do you? Or, worse, into the foursome waiting to tee off the next hole over!

- If your golf shoes aren't already waterproof, apply a weatherproofing spray before the season starts. Trudging around in wet footwear all day will make you very unhappy. Reapply the waterproofing spray periodically according to the manufacturer's directions.

- Rain will affect your shot-making decisions around the course. Wet turf from fairway to green is soft and mushy. That means your drives and iron shots will be shorter and your putts much slower (think of putting on a wet sponge). So be sure to keep the conditions in mind when strategizing about your next shot.

Use Your Equipment Wisely

- Give your towel some cover from the elements. By using the inner metal framework of your umbrella as a rack, you can suspend a towel and keep it dry throughout your round.

- Most golf bags come equipped with a detachable rain cover. Unfortunately, some golfers will immediately chuck it aside after buying the bag. Don't be one of them. Fold up the cover and stow it in one of the bag's pockets. That seemingly useless piece of fabric will keep your clubs, as well as the interior of your bag, dry in case of rain or accidental sprinkler spray.

Worsening Weather

- If you miscalculate, and the rain turns into a lightning storm, call off your game and seek shelter immediately. If a sturdy building is not available, try a car (but not a golf cart). Otherwise, abandon your golf clubs—you don't want to be carrying metal sticks around in an electrical storm—and find a low spot on the ground away from trees, fences, and poles. Squat on the balls of your feet, cover your ears with your hands, and put your head between your knees.

- When you're done playing in the rain, don't stow your equipment in the usual manner. Leave out your shoes and rain suit to dry and be sure to wipe down your clubs—rust can set in if you put them away while wet.

Have Fun!

- Don't focus on the weather. Yes, it's hard to do, but keeping your mind off the rainy conditions will go a long way toward playing better golf. Plus, it'll make you a much more pleasant playing partner!

Playing in the Wind

Most any golf course will have its share of wind at times—some more than others. No matter where you play, knowing how to adapt to breezy conditions can give you an edge over your less savvy playing partners, whose golf balls fly away as if they've grown wings.

Here are some pointers to keep in mind the next time your pants start flapping and the flags turn sideways.

- Don't view the wind as a bad thing. It's part of the game, and it can bring out the best in you. Wind forces you to use your imagination to shape shots. So, fire up your creative juices!

- Don't lean into the wind during your swing. Doing so will encourage a steep swing path, and bad things come from that, notably an open clubface. Squat a bit lower for stability and resist the urge to fight the wind.

- Keep the ball's flight path low. The higher the ball goes, the more influence on it the wind will exert. Makes sense, right? Play the ball about an inch back from normal in your stance and make about a three-quarter swing, really bearing down on the ball. But don't swing steeply. Instead, focus on sweeping the ball forward.

- When playing a crosswind from the tee, set up your ball on the side of the tee box opposite from where the wind is blowing. If playing against a left-to-right wind, tee up on the right side of the box and aim toward the left side of the fairway. Do the opposite for a right-to-left crosswind. This will maximize the amount of room you have to effectively play the wind.

- Headwinds and tailwinds can be dealt with just as effectively. In a headwind, use more club than usual and really try to drive the ball low with that three-quarter swing. For a tailwind, know that you'll need less club because the wind is going to push the ball along with it. Again, keep it low.

- As you get closer to the green, it's best to emulate the Scots, who prefer more of a bump-and-run style of play—and trust me, the originators of links golf respect the power of the wind. Instead of a high pitch or the Phil Mickelson–style flop shot, use a less lofted club to run the ball along the contours of the terrain. Just be sure to analyze those contours beforehand. Just as you would do with a long putt, try to break up the shot into a series of smaller shots that you then join together. Creative, right?

- Yes, a strong wind will influence a putt. Be sure to line up your putt to account for this fact and time your stroke in between gusts, if possible.

Information for Disabled Golfers

Golf is a game for everyone who wants to know the joy of a well-struck shot. In recent years, golf has come a long way toward welcoming those with disabilities. Let's take a look at the available resources.

- First, know that the USGA and the R&A have made provisions within the Rules of Golf to provide an even and equitable playing field for golfers with disabilities. These rules apply to those golfers who are blind; amputees; golfers needing canes, crutches, or wheelchairs; and those with intellectual disabilities. For specifics on these rules modifications, consult the USGA, the R&A, or the Rules of Golf.

- Several organizations promote golf for people with disabilities. A quick visit to their websites will open up a whole world of options. In addition to helping golfers with disabilities play the game, these groups educate professionals, the golf industry, and course owners on their needs. They also provide information on specialized equipment that can make the game much more accessible. Many organize tournaments, too.

+ American Disabled Golfers Association: theadga.com

+ National Amputee Golf Association: www.nagagolf.org

+ National Alliance of Accessible Golf: www.accessgolf.org

- For our men and women in uniform who have suffered traumatic injuries and loss of limbs during their service, golf is still within reach. With the advent of hi-tech prosthetics, specialized equipment, and assistive devices, even those with multiple amputations can still play the game, and play it well. If you or someone you know is a disabled veteran and needs a hand getting back in the game, or wants to take it up for the first time, contact the organizations listed above or your local Disabled American Veterans office (dav.org) for information.

Everyone, regardless of ability or physical challenges, should feel like golf is for them. It's a game that can provide a lifetime of fun and camaraderie, and it's always there to challenge you, from your first round to your last.

Games within the Game

You've probably heard of these games, maybe even played one with your golf buddies or in a charity tournament. Essentially, they're games within the game, and over the years golfers have dreamed up more than a few. In addition to keeping a round of golf interesting, these formats are an equitable way for players of differing abilities to compete against one another. Here's a sampling of the most popular. Try one out this weekend!

Note: Feel free to alter the rules or add new elements when you're out playing with friends. These games are by no means set in stone, unless they're being used as the format for an organized competition. If it's just you and your buddies, get creative—you might even dream up your own game within the game!

Scramble

This format is most popular in tournaments and best suited to foursomes and large groups of golfers. Each foursome plays as a team, with each player teeing off with his or her own ball on each hole. The best of the four tee shots is chosen by the team. All four players will hit the second shot from this spot. As with the tee shot, the best second shot will be chosen as the point from which all team members will hit the third shot. This continues, all the way up to the green until a player holes out. A typical rule is that each team must use four tee shots from each player.

Note: In scramble tournaments, teams will be starting on any of the course's 18 holes. The term "shotgun start" means that all teams tee off at their respective holes at the same time.

Nassau

This game breaks the typical 18-hole round into three matches, with the front nine consisting of one match, the back nine another, and the 18-hole total as the third.

This game is golfer against golfer, and each hole is played as its own match within the match. Still with me? If Player 1 beats Player 2 on a particular hole, Player 1 is considered One Up. If Player 1 wins the next hole, he is Two Up. If the players tie on a hole, it's called "no blood" and the score remains as it did before that hole. The golfer who is Up after nine holes wins that match. The back nine plays the same way. If after 18 holes, the players have tied their two matches, then no one is the winner. If possible, I propose a playoff—winner take all!

Skins

No, there isn't any bodily injury involved here. Think of these skins as points. Eighteen or even nine holes can be played, with the golfers playing against each other. If Player 1 finishes a hole with a par, without being tied or beaten by another player, then Player 1 has won a "skin." If Player 1 wins the hole with a birdie without being tied or beaten, then Player 1 has won two skins. Award three for an eagle win—quite a feat, indeed. If the players tie on a hole, then the skin carries on to the next hole. If three consecutive holes are tied, then the next hole will be worth four skins. At the end of the round, the player with the most skins wins—and probably should buy the drinks at the 19th hole!

Stableford

This is a game of points, and it's a good one to try if your group is pressed for time. It speeds things up because you just pick up your ball and move on if you can't score on a hole. Points are awarded as follows: One point is awarded for a bogey, two for a par, three for a birdie, four for an eagle, and, for a double eagle (albatross), five points! The player with the most points at the end of the round wins.

Stringball

At the start of the round, each player is given one foot of string for every stroke in his or her handicap (for example, a 12-handicap receives 12 feet of string). The player can then use a length of the string to move the ball while in play (out of bad lies, out of hazards, even into the hole). But use the string conservatively. Each time any length is used, that amount is cut off.

Hickory Golf

Over the past decade or so, the golf world has seen a growing movement of players who prefer a "retro" form of the game—known as hickory golf. Players use hickory-shaft clubs from the 19th and early 20th centuries and even dress the part, sporting lots of tweed as well as plus-fours (knickers that extend four inches below the knee), button-down shirts, and ties. Whenever possible, these throwback golfers use antique equipment or purchase reproductions from specialty suppliers. Since the clubs and balls of that era lack the performance characteristics of today's hi-tech versions, play is usually restricted to shorter, older courses, many of which were originally designed for just this type of play. Courses that have become relegated to beginners and quickie after-work players, and those that have seen better days, are witnessing a new wave of interest thanks to these classic golfers.

So if that old layout you've been playing has gotten a bit stale, try taking it on with some 100-year-old equipment! It'll be like playing a entirely new course. Fairway bunkers that were once of no concern off the tee will now seem menacing, and those par-5s will surely turn into colossal feats of skill and patience.

National and international organizations have sprung up to promote hickory golf. They hold tournaments, help players find equipment and repair shops, and foster a community for classic-golf enthusiasts. For more information on this growing niche in the golfing world, check out the Hickory Golf Association, Society of Hickory Golfers, Golf Collectors' Society, and British Golf Collectors Society. All have an online presence.

Popular Betting Games

Care to make things interesting? Here are a sampling of best bets to liven up any round.

Acey Deucey

This one is straightforward, but it's for foursomes only. It's played hole by hole, with the lowest score on a hole being awarded the "ace" and the highest score the "deuce." The ace is paid an agreed-upon amount by the other three players, and the deuce pays an agreed-upon amount to the other three.

Bingo Bango Bongo

Here are the basics of this timeless classic. One point is awarded to the first player on the green (Bingo); one point to the one closest to the pin

(Bango); and one point to the first player to hole out (Bongo). To make it a betting game, assign a dollar value to points. Keep it low—like $1—because for an 18-hole round, there is a total of 54 points to be won (or $54).

Dots

This is a series of side bets agreed upon prior to the start of the round. They can be closest to the pin, longest drive, sand saves, first to hole out, etc. A player who wins one of these side bets is awarded a dot, which he or she places on the scorecard next to the score on that hole. Each dot is assigned a dollar amount. Players settle up at the end of the round based on their dot totals.

Snake

This one's all about putting. First, at the beginning of the round the players determine what the payout will be. During the round, whoever three putts, or more, on a green is given the "snake."

That player will keep the snake until another player three-putts or more on a green. Whoever is left holding the snake at the end of the round pays the other players the agreed-upon amount. A fun twist is to have a toy rubber snake or other item that passes from player to player.

Hazards

Players ante up at the beginning of the round to create a pot. Players must keep track of the number of times they hit into a hazard (sand, water, etc.). The player with the fewest hazards at the end of the round takes the pot.

Pick-up Sticks

Players wager a certain amount for the front nine, the back nine, and the match. Each hole a player loses gives that player the right to remove one of his opponent's clubs from play. The club can be brought back into play if its owner then loses a future hole (or he can take away an opponent's club—but not both!). It's a good idea to give putters immunity. The winner of each set of holes (and ultimately the match) gets the pot.

Scotch Foursome

This is another game for foursomes only. Divide into two pairs. One player in each pair drives the even holes and putts odd, and the other drives odd holes and putts even. The pair who wins gets the pot.

Golf and Kids

Whether they're your children, your grandchildren, or your nieces and nephews, passing along your golf knowledge can be immensely rewarding and will ensure this wonderful game has a future. Here are some things to keep in mind when introducing the game to the little ones.

1. **Keep in mind who your audience is.** Remember, these are kids, not your weekend golfing buddies. So keep it light and don't sweat every little thing. It's important for them to have fun! If they don't, then they won't play.

2. **Talk about the game.** Tell them about the history, stories of past champions, and, most of all, the camaraderie and competitive spirit. Describe the pastoral beauty found on the golf course and the fun of watching a perfectly hit shot find its mark. Tell them why you love the game, and why you think they might come to love it, too.

3. **Introduce them to the equipment.** Take out your golf bag and explain what each piece is for. Let them try swinging the clubs. Don't get hung up on grip, stance, and all the techinicalities and proper technique. Just let them be kids and explore something new.

4. **Demonstrate the basics.** If you've got some old clubs lying around, cut one or two down to kid size; try an inexpensive regrip kit. Then, the next time you hit the driving range, bring along the children and their clubs. Show them the fundamentals and then let them swing away. Don't get too involved in mechanics; just give a few pointers and let them be.

5. **If they show an interest, pick up a set of kids' clubs.** Shop around at yard sales or used sporting goods stores. Buying new is great, but kids grow out of them quickly or might lose interest. Buy used, and you won't be out much dough either way.

6. **When you think the time is right, take them out to a nine-hole par-3 course.** Go late in the day when it isn't crowded. This way, there's no pressure of people watching, and they can knock the ball about to their heart's content.

7. **Most important, be a good role model.** Watch your language, don't throw your clubs, and follow the rules and etiquette. Show them it's a game of honor and respect. And be patient.

Walk or Ride: The Age-Old Dilemma

Most courses these days, at least those in the United States, offer motorized golf carts for rent. (Rentals are not as popular in the British Isles.) Whether you want to walk or ride is probably one of the first questions you'll be asked when checking in at the pro shop. Here's some advice regarding both options.

The Benefits of Walking

- Walking is how the game was originally played. So, if you're a purist, it's the way to go. It's also good for you.

- Walking the course will allow you to take in all the sights and sounds the layout has to offer. This is especially important if you're visiting a new course. Walking up to your ball will help you get the lay of the land a lot better than speeding down the cart path.

- Walking is a great way to burn off stress and frustration. A stroll up to your ball, along with some deep breaths, can help you shake off a terrible shot.

The Benefits of Riding

- Walking can be tiresome, however. If you're older or have mobility issues, taking a cart will probably be best. And, no matter your age or health, if you're in for a long round on a busy course, it's really nice to have a place to sit to wait out the group ahead.

- Speaking of busy courses: if the majority of the other golfers are using carts on a busy course, it's probably best to follow suit. If you're one of the few groups walking while everyone else is riding, then be prepared for folks asking to play through your group *all* day.

- If you're playing in extreme heat and humidity and you're not used to such conditions, you should probably pony up the extra dollars and ride. Even if you're using a push/pull cart while walking, a few hours baking in the sun will do a number on you. Plus, a golf cart will give you the ability to carry extra water. In this case, riding in a cart will make for a much more enjoyable round, and it could save you from heat exhaustion!

Note: Whether you walk or ride, be sure to keep play moving along. And try to keep pace with the group in front. If the group behind you is on your heels all afternoon, allow them to play through. It's just good etiquette.

Resources

Whether you want golf instruction, news of the pros, equipment reviews, travel destinations, or the latest in golf fashion, there is an organization, magazine, or website to help you.

American Disabled Golfers Association
www.theadga.com

American Junior Golf Association
www.ajga.org

Ladies' Professional Golf Association
www.lpga.com

National Alliance of Accessible Golf
www.accessgolf.org

National Amputee Golf Association
www.nagagolf.org

Professional Golfers' Association of America
www.pga.com

The R&A
www.randa.org

United States Golf Association
www.usga.org

Magazines

Golfweek
www.golfweek.com

Golf Digest
www.golfdigest.com

Golf Magazine
www.golf.com

Golf Tips
www.golftipsmag.com

Kingdom Magazine
www.arnieskingdom.com

LINKS Magazine
www.linksmagazine.com

Websites

ESPN Golf
www.espn.go.com/golf

Golf Channel
www.golfchannel.com

Ladies European Tour
www.ladieseuropeantour.com

PGA of America
www.pga.com

PGA Tour
www.pgatour.com

PGA European Tour
www.europeantour.com

Sports Illustrated: Golf
www.si.com/golf

MyScorecard
www.myscorecard.com

World Golf Championships
www.worldgolfchampionships.com

Acknowledgments

I would like to thank Brian Aalto and Rick Hamilton for teaching me many of the things featured in this book. And, of course, a big thank-you to the playing partners who have patiently endured a round with me.